Autobiographical Poems

BY

John F McMullen

Autobiographical Poems

Copyright 2023 John F McMullen

Forward

This book had its genesis on October 28, 2023 when I was privileged to be one of the three *"Featured Poets"* at the monthly online meeting of the **Brownstone Poets**, a well-known New York City poetry group. In preparation for the event, I gathered a number of poems, autobiographical in nature, and then winnowed them down to the allocated 15-minute time slot.

After reviewing the poems, I realized that, with the addition of some other poems, I could put together a book that would reflect not only my life in poetry but also my love of sports and my extreme luck at every stage of my adult life – and that is this book.

As always, I must mention my late parents, Jack and Clara McMullen, my older brother the late Robert McMullen, the best person I have ever known, my loving wife of 45 years, Barbara McMullen, and my children, Claire McMullen Cleary and Luke McMullen. Without them, this wonderful ride would not have been possible.

The journey to poetry would never have been possible without the encouragement of two old friends, the late Jacqueline Wolf Birch and George Hopkins, and the literary nourishment I found in the Hudson Valley Writers Center and the Mahopac Writers Group.

The initial poem in the book, *"Bukowski & Me"*, explains my unlikely movement into poetry and the following one, *"Cashing A Check"*, is the first I had published. I have included one prose piece, *"Teddy Ballgame and My Brother"* because it seemed to fit.

To the reader – thank you for taking the time to read this book; comments are always welcome to johnmac13@gmail.com

Table of Contents

Bukowski & Me

By John F McMullen

I have told this story
many times before
but will do it again
I just tell stories
(*and call it poetry*)
I never liked poetry
although I studied it as
an English Literature
major in college
I never saw the point
I was a published writer
      a reporter
      a columnist
      a reviewer
      an author of books
over 2,500 pieces
but not a poet

Not a writer of poetry
not even a reader of poetry
for thirty-five years
since then:
> thousands of poems written
> hundreds of them published in magazines
> ten books or chapbooks published
> bookcases full of poetry books

what changed all of this is my life?

I was coming out of a rest-room
in a Barnes & Noble
and walking down an aisle
when I saw a book with
a very strange title
I picked it up and
took it back to my table

It was a book of poetry!
by Charles Bukowski
I read it anyway
I was doomed

I recognized immediately
that Bukowski was:
> an alcoholic
> a misogynist
> more than a bit of a nut
> fucking brilliant

and he made me want to try my hand
and so I did

If you dislike my writing
blame Bukowski
(*he used profanity too*)
if you like it, then,
say a prayer for his
eternal soul
(*you might include
mine as well*)

Cashing A Check

I just saw this wonderful line
in a column in a motorcycle
magazine:
*The mind writes checks that
the body can't cash*.*

The vision that many from the
old neighborhood have of me is
short and thin with a Pepsi in
one hand and a cigarette
in the other

Others will remember me as
taller and thin, hitting a jumper
from the corner or throwing
a "no-look pass" to a cutter.

Others will picture me at the
end of the bar in the Broadstone
with an open pack of Pall Malls and
a half-finished beer on the bar;
Don Gibson's "I Can't Stop Loving You"
on the jukebox.
Pat, one more when you get a chance

Age has taken the jumper
Diabetes has taken the Pepsi
Common Sense has taken the
cigarette and booze.

I am older and wiser and
hopefully more tolerant
I am satisfied with my life

but

to just be able to once more
fake the man guarding me and
go up with a jumper and
get nothing but net

To be able to, once more,
"cash that check"

*"Milestones" by Robert Rasor, American Motorcyclist; March 2006

Grandparents

My four grandparents came from Ireland,
young and unmarried, to the United States.
My mother's parents went to Charlestown, MA
where they met, married, and had children.
My father's parents did the same in New York.

I never knew three of them;
only my father's mother survived into
my memory (and I never really liked her).
but what courage they must have had.

Would I have been able to pick up,
leave family and friends behind and
sail off on a coffin ship across an ocean?

I doubt it
-- but I certainly owe them.

Jack

John Washington McMullen
Dates
July 25, 2021
was the 117th Anniversary
of my father's birth on
July 25, 1904
on March 11, 1951
he died after slipping
on ice at the age of 46

I had less time with
my father than with
 my mother (*40 years*)
 my wife (*43 years and still counting*)
 my brother (*64 years*) ... and
 my children, Claire and Luke *(51 and 48 years, respectively, still*
counting)
only 11 years
but he stands out very clearly
in my mind

At birth
he was baptized
Washington John McMullen
after a wealthy friend of the family
who was to leave a good
deal of money for him in trust
(*a deal later reneged on by*
his much younger widow)

He hated the name
his cousins called him *Washy*
and sometime between
1920 and 1930 according
to the US Census he flipped it
to *John Washington McMullen*

It must have been a legal flip
because his official name
as an NYPD police officer was
John Washington McMullen
and he was always *Jack* anyhow
He grew up in the first elevator
apartment house in the Yorkville
section io New Your City and was
neighbors and friends with ex-NYC
Mayor Bob Wagner and his father
a United States Senator
Along the way he was the
captain of the Regis high
school basketball team
(*a position later held by*
Dr. Anthony Fauci)

He became a Wall Street
Account Executive and
married my mother and
my older brother was born

All was moving along well
until the *Great Depression*
wiped out the firm and he
joined the family business NYPD

And I was born

When I was three my brother
joined an order of Christian
Brothers with my father telling
him that *the door was always open*
if you ever want to come home

So, my parents really
raised two only children
and I had their full attention
my mother was a stay-at-home
mom and my father was
      funny
      a great storyteller
      a constant reader
      generous to a fault
      a real sports fan
and we had a comfortable life

He was a New York Giant baseball fan
as well as a New York Yankee and
Giant and Yankee football one
(*there was a Yankee football team then*)
fan and took me to the games of all
I'm sure he got game NYPD passes and
remember he got to go to the front of the line
at Babe Ruth's wake at Yankee Stadium
in August 1948 (*I thought that the perk
was fine then but not really later*)

And then less than three years later
my whole life changed when he died.
my mother moved to Washington
and went off to work
and I went off to military school

I think of him often particularly
on July 25th and March 11
his many good points
and the fact that he often
bought too many drinks
for himself and others

But he was a tough
Irish-American cop
living in Inwood
the neighborhood
with more bars than
any neighborhood
in New York City
(*Walter Winchell*
called it "Ginwood)
And that was part of
the life in those days

I wish that he had lived
long enough for us
to sit in a bar over
a couple of beers and talk

Clara

Clara Crilley McMullen
My mother
born on All Saints Day
November 1 1901
gave her birth date
as November 1 1904
so she would appear
younger than my father
who was born on
July 25, 1904
She worked outside
the house when
I was very young but
I only really
remembered her
as a stay-at-home
loving wife and mother
until

my father died in
an accident on
March 11 1951

then she picked
herself up and
went back to work
becoming the only
support of herself
and a fairly wild child
When this wild child
grew up a little and
would come home
at night after trying
to drink up all the beer
in the neighborhood

I would light a cigarette
before entering the
apartment thinking
that the smoke would
cover the alcohol smell
She would sit across the
room from me and have
a conversation for a while
and then go off to bed
never asking me if I had
been drinking

Years later she told me
that the smoke carried
the beer smell across
the room to her so
she never had to
ask the question

In her final years
she lived in a
nursing home
on the banks of
the Hudson River

She was in a state of confusion believing that
       the Hudson was the Charles River where she grew up
       my brother Robert was her late older brother Frank
       I was her long dead brother John
but
when I had my children with me
       they were her grandchildren
       and I was her son
the mind is a very funny thing
She died on
New Year's Eve 1980
she was a wiser woman
than I ever realized and
I owe her a lot

Bud

Robert John McMullen
always called *Buddy* or *Bud*
was the best person
that I ever knew
a model of Christian Charity.

He was a college professor
for over forty years,
a Christian Brother of Ireland for
twenty-five,
a married man for over
twenty-five years
and a gentle person
for all his seventy years on earth,
the last decade of which he was racked
with terrible Alzheimer's.

He taught me in two courses
while I was in college
(*two well-deserved A's –
and threw me out of class once*)
and taught me
in other ways for all my life
he was my brother

Kevin

Kevin Paul Buckley
my oldest friend
a year and a half younger
both from
254 Seaman Avenue
in Inwood, Manhattan.
New York, New York

He a Brooklyn Dodger Fan
me a Boston Red Sox one
we played ball together
roamed Inwood Park together
hung out in each other's
apartments and talked
about everything

Then his parents
kidnapped him away
to Larchmont in the
foreign province of
Westchester County

In spite of the distance
we stayed close
even after my father died
through
      letter writing
      phone calls
      bike trips
      sleepovers

Then we drifted a bit
>I was a commuter to Iona College
>he was a resident at Yale
>I moved into the world of computers
>he became a foreign correspondent
>I married and moved 5 miles from 254
>he went to Vietnam for Newsweek
>I read his stories
>he didn't understand what I did

Then he was back
first to Harvard
then to New York
and we picked
up again – still
in somewhat
different worlds

Then I divorced and
remarried to the
wonderful Barbara
and he married the
wonderful Gail

And then he,
a technophobe,
needed computer
instruction to
write articles
and his first book
and Barbara
became his tutor

(Note – when his
publisher told him
that his book was
too long and he must
cut 15 pages he
became almost suicidal
until Barbara showed
him how to shrink the
margins keeping the
book intact – and
it worked!)

(Note II – when an
editor completely
ruined a piece
that I wrote on
technology changing
the whole thrust of the
article and I called
him for advice
he asked are there
any factual errors
in the revised piece?
when I admitted
that there were not
he said simply
cash the check
and I did)
and we went
on like this
many phone calls
terrific parties at
his apartment   .

UNTIL

he had a stroke!
a stroke that
worsened over
many years

There were
still phone calls
but less and not
as involved

In the summer
of 2021 he
(*or Gail for him*)
wrote a blurb for
the back cover
of my latest book

In November 2021
it was over
expected but
still a shock.

The Neighborhood Culture

I was born and raised
in the Inwood section
at the very top
of Manhattan Island

It was an Irish Catholic /Jewish section then
Each group thought that the neighborhood
belonged to them
and they were both right

It had three claims to fame then:
a giant park with a large real forest,
Columbia University's football stadium,
and more bars than any neighborhood in NYC

People came from all over to
watch football, play in the park, and drink in the bars
Walter Winchell called it "GinWood"
in the press and on the radio

The legal drinking age in NY was 18 then
so we could start in the park at 15 or 16
When I first tasted beer, I didn't like it;
that soon changed!

We moved to the bars at 17 or 18
Whether in the park or in the bars,
the beer was merely the catalyst;
it was the conversation that bonded us

I no longer imbibe
In the words of the great sportswriter Jimmy Cannon,
"I stopped drinking twenty-five years ago;
I retired with the title"

I knew a number who fell into the bottle;
most, however, did not
We became engineers, lawyers, accountants,
writers, and technologists

Were it not for half quart cans of Pabst
and the advent of the desktop computer,
I would never have become a writer

So I owe a lot to the neighborhood and the culture
I go back once a month for a luncheon
There are now very few bars
The neighborhood is Dominican at one end
and gentrified and expensive at the other

The times and stores may be different
but the friendships and memories live on
My Inwood is now a *state of the mind*!
Who's got the church key"

The Little Black Boy

When I was just 11,
a little white boy,
a little black boy
changed my life

I grew up in an Irish /
Jewish neighborhood -
that is understating it
there were few Italians,
less Jews, and almost no
Protestants and NO blacks.

I heard about blacks -- I
cheered for Jackie Robinson
and didn't see what the big
deal was -- Why didn't they
always let them play?

But I also heard the terms
that we now know as racist -
"coon", "boogie", and, of
course, "the N word"

But I didn't see any of this
as a big deal either -- we
called each other "shanty",
"lace curtain", "stupid micks",
etc.

Then I went to a Catholic
grammar school track meet
outside my neighborhood
-- at night
I had to fight to get my
parents to let me go.

So, I'm standing in a line
-- a long line -- for a soda
and this little black kid
about eight years old
was being a real pain
in the ass
jumping all around
making noise
behaving like, well,
an 8 year-old.

Finally, he stepped on my toes
I grabbed him by his shoulders,
shook him, and pushed him,
saying
"Get out of here, you little
nigger"

He ran off, crying
I was still in line
when he came back
with his big brother

I immediately knew
that it was all over
-- these guys carry knives
I was dead.

He came up to me and
said
"Did you call my brother
a nigger?"
I gulped and said
"Yes"

He looked at me harshly
and said
"You're a Catholic;
you should know better"
.. and walked away

And, from then on,
I knew better

(If he has just
"kicked the shit out of me",
as I expected, all I would
have learned was to
"look for the big brother first")

Rock and Roll-- 1955

I rush in, turn the radio on,
and tune to 1010AM – WINS,
just in time to hear the sound of
Cozy Eggleston's "Big Heavy"
and Alan Freed is on the air!

Freed transformed music for me
and my contemporaries.
We closed the door on our parents'
Sinatra, Bennett, and Peggy Lee
(only to re-open it years later)
and brought in "The Fat Man
from New Orleans", Clyde, Chuck,
Roy, Bo, Ray, The Clovers, Smiley,
Shirley and Lee, and most of all
the DUWOP sound.

We ate it up, becoming music junkies;
We knew that Curtis Williams was the
lead singer of the Penguins;
Tony Williams, the lead of the Platters;
and Otis Williams of the Charms and
that none were related.

We, white kids all, moved deeper into the
black culture, going to shows at New York's
famed Apollo Theatre in Harlem (and then
across the street to Clyde McPhatter's record
store) and we moved from the white Freed to
the black Jocko Henderson on WADO who
taught us to rhyme:
 "Ee tiddy ock,
this is the Jock,
saying oh poppa do
and how do you do?"

And we learned to identify songs
from the very first sounds
(this was a big help to those of
us who only did slow dances and
could have been fooled by songs
like "Blue Jean Bop" and "From the
Bottom of My Heart" which started
slow and went to fast)

"BaDo BaDo" (Moonglows)
"OohWaWa OohWaWa" (Nutmegs)
"ShoDo and ShoobyDo" (Five Satins)
"AWopBobALooALopBamBoom" (Little Richard)
"HeyDoMotADo OohWa OohWa" (TeenAgers)
"TiSiMookaBoomDiAy TiSiMookaBoomDiAy" (Five Keys)
"Liddle Liddle Liddle Yeah" (Cleftones)

and then Elvis came along and drove
the white girls crazy and the parents nuts
but it was still ok – as it was with other
Sun Record stars, Johnny, Carl, Roy, and
the incomparable Jerry Lee.

But then the awful white singers began
to emerge and be played more and more,
Tab Hunter, Fabian, Frankie Avalon and
it was much so we found WNEW, returning
to Sinatra and friends, or moved to Jazz, only
to be liberated again by The Beetles, Dylan,
and the Byrds.

And we found out that our original music guide.
Alan Freed, had taken "payola" to play songs
and taken credit for writing songs which he
had nothing to do with.

So we grew slightly jaded and loved songs
with lines like:
"the three men I admire most,
the Father, Son, and Holy Ghost,
*They caught the last train for the coast."**

* From "American Pie" by Don McLean

The Friday Night Dance

On Friday night, we'd get
suited up and head down to
our local Catholic Grammar School
for a teen age dance
(when we got a bit older,
we'd kill a ½ pint of
Old Mr. Boston Lemon
Flavored Vodka first)

I'd be wrapped around a girl
In a slow dance, my hand caressing
her hair as my torso tried to join hers
when Father Devine would wander
over and say
"Leave room for the Holy Ghost"

That statement might gave opened up
space between some other bodies
but I would make the point that
*"the Holy Ghost is spiritual, Father;
he can fit anywhere he wants"*
(fifty years later, after winning a Silver
Star as a Vietnam chaplain, he still
remembers those remarks)

If a young lady returned after such a dance
to dance again, she had to really like me
for I would have been singing in her ear
with the worst singing voice in the world.

Oh, well; it was prior to the pill and
these girls didn't put out anyhow.
… so we drank.

Six Months Wonder

I was too young
for Korea
although I had a friend
whose older brother died there.

I was too old
for Vietnam
although I had friends
whose younger brothers died there.

I was working as a civilian
For the Department of the Army
and there was pressure to get my
"military obligation" out of the way.

So, I spent from November 1962
through May 1963 in Fort Dix, NJ
and Fort Sill, Oklahoma
as a six months wonder.

I hated it!
It was boring, repetitious and
an awful lot of "chickenshit".
I wanted to get on with my life!

It was only later that
I got to realize
how much I learned
in just those few months.

The Irish Catholic from NYC
worked with the Protestant
from Alabama who thought
that the Pope was a heretic.

The College English Major
found common ground
with high school dropouts
who thought reading was
a big waste of time.

The local basketball
gym rat and fanatic
found the same teamwork
as part of an artillery crew.

The kid from the lily-white
neighborhood of Inwood
saw his black platoon buddies
suffer bigotry and exclusion
in Lawton, OK.

The tedium of spit-shining
shoes and cleaning a rifle
with a toothbrush made
me "do things right".

It was only much later that I found
the answer to my constant question
"what is this 'good training' for?"
The answer was *"for life"*!

Lawton 1963

I was in the Army at Fort Sill, OK
in what then seemed a colossal waste of time
but, in retrospect, was really
a very important part of my life.

The town adjacent to Fort Sill, Lawton
had no industry
but it did have
bars, clip joints, hookers, and whatever
else could separate a soldier from his money.

It also had
an Indian section,
a Mexican section,
a black section,
a white soldier section,
and a white real people's section.

In New York City,
we had "neighborhoods"
Italian neighborhoods,
Jewish neighborhoods,
Irish neighborhoods,
Black neighborhoods.

But we never thought
of New York City as segregated.
(Maybe we should have.)
But Lawton was
definitely segregated!

Anyway, my platoon had
an "IG Inspection"
and did exceptionally well.

My platoon Sergeant,
a very sharp soldier,
who I respected,
gathered us together
and said:
"I'm proud of you.
You did very well.
The Supply Sergeant and I
just bought a bar a mile out of town.
Come on down.
The first one's on me."

No dope, he!
If we started drinking
a mile from nowhere,
we were there to stay.

As anyone knowing us
might expect,
Warren (from the old neighborhood)
and I were the first ones
from our unit to arrive.

I was into around my third beer
when Bob (also from Inwood)
walked in with two other folks,
both black.

The bartender saw me greet them
and said to me
"*I can't serve those folks*".
(It was obvious that he meant
the black folks).

I explained that my sergeant
owned this place and
invited his unit down for a beer
and that these folks were
part of the unit.

No good!
The bartender said that
*"they should have known that
the invitation didn't include them"*.

That, of course, set me off and I
was soon as persona non-grata
as my black friends.
Out in the parking lot, I said
"Ok – where can we get a drink together?"
-- only to be told,
"No place in this town"
So "they" went to "their bars"
and Bob, Warren, and I went to "ours."

I was reluctant to say anything
to my platoon sergeant.
He was, after all, my superior.

But, four weeks later,
after I was transferred to another unit,
I was sitting in a bar with a book
and a pitcher of beer –
not an unusual sight
when Sgt. Jones came in the door.

I waved him over to my table,
poured him a beer,
and told him the story.
He said *"I feel terrible.
I hate to cause anyone
to be embarrassed"*
Great! He wouldn't let
it happen again in his bar!

But he added *"We really
don't mix down here"*.
I plunged right in.
*"What do you think of
Sgt. Lowery* (his black superior)?"
"He's a fine soldier and a gentleman."
"Would you have a beer with him?"
"I have in the NCO club. He's good company".

Undaunted (and not knowing when to quit),
I went on.
"Would you have him to your house?"
He looked at me as though I was
bereft of my senses.
"I have a wife and daughter".

I had no idea what to say.
I mumbled something,
changed the subject,
finished my beer,
and went on my way.

That was forty-six years ago.
Things have changed greatly.
Barack Obama has commanded
the armed forces
but
are we all different?
I hope so.

The Fork In The Road

The great philosopher, L.P. Berra,
known to his friends and fans as Yogi,
has had many memorable expressions:
"No one goes there any more; it's too crowded";
"It gets late early out there" (referring to the
left field shadows at Yankee Stadium);
"It ain't over 'til it's over";
and many more.

My favorite of all is
"When you come to the fork in the road, take it."

To me, this bit of wisdom has always meant –
-- when faced with a decision, make it!
sometimes, the forks aren't clearly marked
and I have been very lucky in the paths
which I chose to wander down.

It was a Saturday morning 60 years ago
I was driving a friend for us to take a government test
only because he asked me to -- doing this led me
eventually into a fifty-year career with computers,
something I knew nothing about at the time
and in which I had zero interest.

"When you come to the fork in the road, take it."

Years later, I made a presentation to a potential
client and, while we didn't make a sale, I became
very impressed with the female member of the
evaluation team. Seven years later, I received a
call from a client asking if I knew the same woman
who was now applying for a job at the firm.

I strongly recommended her, she got the job, and
coincidentally, I joined the same firm shortly thereafter.
that was forty-four years ago;
although it meant us both
leaving over 10-year marriages
and changing career paths
we've been married for forty-four years

"When you come to the fork in the road, take it."

We were starting our own consulting business
working with large computer systems – *Mainframes*
but when a friend saw us standing by an elevator
and came over to wish us luck
he asked if we had
seen the computer on Ben Rosen's desk

We hadn't – and didn't know who
Ben Rosen was but we went off
to see him in the Research Department
he was the Electronics Analyst and
the computer was an Apple II
it didn't do much but I bought one
to try to see how these new devices
could work in our new business

Two months later
the first spreadsheet ever – VisiCalc
was introduced and we had an early copy
there was tremendous demand for training
we were the only game in town
and our business changed totally
from a mainframe consulting business
to concentrate on the new world
of personal computing

"When you come to the fork in the road, take it."

The connection with Ben Rosen
now a good friend paid off when he invited
us to a conference in Lake Geneva WI
and we met the developers of VisiCalc
Dan Bricklin and Bob Frankston

When returning from an upstate NY
consulting job we stopped for dinner
at a restaurant -- Plumbush's
there was only one other party
in the dining room – an older couple

When I heard one mention Apple
I jumped in and we talked about computing
as the conversation ended he told me
that I should join the Apple User Group in NYC
and told me about all that it did
so I did
and wound up becoming its President for 9 years

"When you come to the fork in the road, take it."

And because of our connections there
(*Barbara was the Secretary*)
a Dean at NYU asked us to teach a course
and that led to us over the last 43 years
teaching at 10 colleges between us

"When you come to the fork in the road, take it."

I

In the meantime
an editor at Popular Computing Magazine
asked Dan Bricklin to write an article
about how business people used VisiCalc
he demurred but suggested that the editor
speak to Barbara McMullen
who knew more about this than anyone
he did and while we had no plans
to be writers
we've been writing for publication for 40 years

"When you come to the fork in the road, take it."

Even though I was an English Literature major
and read constantly – fiction and non-fiction
and wrote constantly for magazines and newspapers
I had no interest in poetry – had neither written
any nor read any for 35 years

However
one day walking down an aisle in Barnes and Noble
I came across a book with a strange tittle
I took it off the shelf and back to my table
it was by a fellow named Charles Bukowski
I opened it --- and saw it was poetry
although my reaction was Ugh! I read some of it
and felt *that Bukowski was an alcoholic, a
misogynist, and crazed – but also brilliant*

I also decided that
if this lunatic can do this I can too
that was fifteen years ago
Now I have
        hundreds of poems published in magazines, journals, and anthologies
        ten books of poetry published
and am the Poet Laureate of a 36,000-citizen town in Westchester NY

"When you come to the fork in the road, take it."

Many paths
many choices to be made
a wonderful life

I took the fork in the road

Past and Future

I recently did a retrospective
for a poetry feature
based on the theme
"*A Fork In The Road*"

In it, I tried to address
how I got from
an apartment-dwelling
city denizen
working on Wall Street
as a technology executive
to someone
      living in the "boonies"
      with a wife, 2 cats and a dog
      feeding squirrels, birds, chipmunks, deer, & groundhogs
      and writing poetry
This analysis,
a study in making a plan
and then having life happen
led me to narrow the possible
reasons for me being here
to the real answer:
I fell head-over-heels in love
with a Philadelphia Princess
who always wanted a barn

Now that I understand the past
I can move on to the future
but since I can't know
     how long the future will be
     will there be accidents or illness
     what will happen in the country or world
     will we have enough income to continue as present
I'll just have to ride it out and see what happens
Plans don't work anyhow

The Other Path

I have written about
The Fork In The Road
thinking about it more
I realized that many
in my experience have
come to the fork and
taken a brand new path

My father Jack McMullen
was an account executive
with a brokerage firm
until the tail end of
the Great Depression
and then became a
hotel detective until
he followed his
father's path and
became an NYPD
officer and detective

My brother Robert McMullen
was a member of a
religious order for 25 years
(*he taught me in college*
and later was the Principal
of the school at which a
young Ferdinand Lewis Alcindor
later Kareem Abdul-Jabbar
starred in basketball)
He then left the order
married and continued
teaching in college
for another 25

The mother of my children
Patricia McCarroll
rather than go back
to teaching after our divorce
went to law school
worked for a few firms
and then joined the
federal government

My wife of 43 years
Barbara McMullen
and I left corporate
careers to follow
a path together as
       technology consultants
       writers
       college teachers
       even poets

My daughter
Claire Cleary McMullen
a marathon runner
and the winner of various
New York mini-marathons
left a successful career as
a marketing executive
at the ago of 40 to become
a physical trainer

My son Luke McMullen
broke the mold by
deciding in high school
that he was going to
write for television
and the movies

After college he
followed his muse and
went off to Hollywood
and has supported
himself since
(*he did expand his
portfolio by moving
himself also into
game scripting but that
expands the path rather
than leaving it*)

What to make of all this?
I don't really know
but just point out
that the entire cast
showed a lot of
self confidence
and courage.

Barbara

I first met Barbara
when as an officer of a
technology consulting firm
I made a presentation to
the firm where she worked

She struck me as being
extremely sharp and
when the other
two people from her firm
and two from mine
had lunch I made sure
that I sat next to her

That was the last that
I saw of her
for seven years
in the meantime
we sold my firm
to a larger one and
I became responsible
for all computer system
installations at the new
much larger firm

One of the firms that
we installed a large system
at was a very prestigious
Wall Street firm
(Morgan Stanley) and
I was personally involved
with the installation

About a year after the
system was installed
I got a call from the
person in charge of
Morgan Stanley's
computer systems
to ask me if I had
ever heard of a
person whose resume
he had just received

It was the same woman
that I remembered from
seven years before!

I had no contact with
here in all that time
but had asked about her
when I met people
from her firm and
always received
good reports and
therefore I gave her
a glowing reference

When I heard that she
had accepted the position
and started her new job
I called her to congratulate
her and she thanked me
but called me *Tom*

Three months later
I was offered an
executive position
at Morgan Stanley
and accepted it

In my first
three months in
the new position
I spent a good
deal of time in
San Francisco
overseeing the
operational
take-over of a
firm acquired by
Morgan Stanley

In the late Autumn
I was back in
New York full
time and my only
interaction with
Barbara was
the office and
relating to business

On December 8th
in the late afternoon
we were forced out
of our offices by a
bomb scare and
after milling around
the lobby many
moved to a nearby pub
and for the first time
in seven years
I sat at a table
with Barbara

On December 27th
I told her that I
wanted to spend
the rest of my life
with her

It took until the
following May 12th
for us to finally
begin our total
lives together
a move that took
great

       courage
       commitment
       naivete
       confidence
       love

because
       we were both leaving marriages of over 10 years
       we were jeopardizing well developing careers
we did it anyhow

That was forty-four years ago
since then we have together:
       helped raise two terrific children
       had a consulting business that took us to 14 states, DC, Puerto Rico,
and   Mexico
       taught in ten different colleges and universities
       written 10 books and contributed to encyclopedias and anthologies
       written countless newspaper and magazine columns
       published hundreds of poems
       been active in technology and writing organization and performed
community service
and always been in love

Barbara Ludman McMullen
I love you

What Did He Expect?

God. many believe, made us
in "His image and likeness",
(or so I was taught in
Catholic grammar school).

But he didn't really.
He built some "fuck-up"
into us and then had us
populate through incest.
That was a good recipe
for real success!

He gave Adam & Eve everything
-- including curiosity and then
pointed out an apple and said
"Don't eat it."
What did he expect?

He gave men cocks
and women cunts
and built in a hunger
to use them … and
then proscribed how,
when, and with who
they could be used.
What did he expect?

He demolished two
towns for "immoral
behavior" and told
a group not to turn
around and look.
What did he expect?

God told us to love
each other and worship
Him – and then gave
different rules to different
groups, letting each think
that they had the truth.
-- Don't eat pork
-- Don't eat beef
-- Keep holy Friday
-- Keep holy Saturday
-- Keep holy Sunday
-- Jesus Christ was God
-- Jesus Christ wasn't God
-- The Pope is God's Representative
-- The Pope is the Devil's Whore
-- Mohammad is God's Prophet
-- Mohammad was a con man
-- Don't say My Holy Name
-- Use My Name Often In Prayer
and so the zealots killed (and
continue to kill) each other.
What did He expect?

And now less and less
educated people say
that they believe in Him!
What did He expect?

God's Musings

I threw Adam out of the Garden;
I turned women into pillars of salt;
I flooded the earth;
I gave them different ways to worship me –
-- so they would kill each other over the best way;
I even named a group my "Chosen People' –
-- so every one would hate them;
I had my messenger say "Turn the other cheek" –
-- so they could crucify him;
I set off volcanoes;
I sent tsunamis;
and, in between, famine and plagues.

I've done every godammed thing I could
do to these insignificant bastards –
-- but the fuckers don't give up!

Which Would You Choose?

Let's see now ...

God wants you to remain chaste,
worship Him regularly,
particularly on a day off
(often after a long night out).

The Devil advises you to
fuck and such as often as possible
and to sleep in on Sundays
(hopefully with last night's partner).

If you follow God's directive,
you will go to Heaven
(if there is a Heaven;
if there is a God).

If you follow the Devil's,
you'll take the Downbound Train
(if there is a Hell;
if there is a Devil).

Which will you choose?
(a bird in the hand?)

Damned If I Know

I find myself
ending more
than one poem
with the words
"Damned if I know".

Upon reflection,
I realize how many
facts that I know
and how little I
really understand
about the things
that matter.

I know who played
third base for the
1927, 1939, and 1949
Yankees, who developed
the first spreadsheet, who
played Matt Dillon on the
radio, who held the New
York Knicks single game
scoring record before
Bernard King, what the
first graphic browser was,
who wrote "Sincerely", who
played the leprechaun in the
original "Finian's Rainbow",
and who replaced Clyde
McPhatter as the lead singer
of the Dominos.

Yet, I cannot say for sure if
there really is a God, whether
or not there is an afterlife,
whether there will ever be true
peace in the world, and really,
what has been the purpose of my life.

So I know a lot
and
understand very little.

I Was A Basketball Whore

I played in the park
I played CYO ball
I played for an Episcopal Church
I played in a league at the Jewish Y
I played Intramural Ball in College
I was the proverbial "gym rat"
in college playing between classes
and often when I should have been in class

I went to Iona College,
I really majored in *"Basketball and Beechmont"*
The Beechmont is the bar across the street
from the college
Hey – I'm from Inwood

I grew up small and only grew late in college
I was a good ballplayer, then for a while,
a very good player, then a pretty good player,
then a good player again, and finally, an "OK player"
when I finally stopped in my mid '50s
I played in leagues on Wall Street
I played in "Open Leagues" around Manhattan and the Bronx
I played in leagues in Westchester
and -- "pickup" for two hours most Sunday mornings.

Now, I have regular cortisone shots in my hips and knees,
I've had minor surgery in both knees --
-- and then jelly pumped into them.
No cartilage in my knees or ankles and
arthritis all through my back, hips, knees and ankles
-- and my right ankle brings a limp and constant pain.
If the most recent shot and 24/7 brace doesn't work,
then it's fusion or a replacement – not a happy scenario

My orthopedist, an old player himself,
says that it's all from basketball.
If I had known then,
back in my basketball days,
what I know now
I wouldn't have changed a fucking thing.

Lawrence Peter

Lawrence Peter Berra
"Yogi" to most
is as known for his
supposed misstatements
as his baseball prowess

Yet I see his famous statements
as brilliance and metaphor
perhaps made with a
limited vocabulary
(*Yogi, due to his immigrant*
family upbringing and
World War II service did not
have much formal education,
leaving school after the 8th grade)

My favorite one
I've written a poem about it is
"*When you come to the fork in the road., take it*"
to me, this means "Make a decision
and follow it – don't freeze!"
and I have made them
and luckily, made the right ones

Another famous one is
"*It ain't over till it's over*"
 Good advice for any competition
      sport
      legal
      politics
play it right to the end!

Some seem confusing
until you think about them
"No one goes there nowadays, it's too crowded"
We all know good restaurants that have
gotten so popular that the food isn't worth the wait
"It gets late early out there"
(referring to left field at Yankee Stadium)
The Stadium shadows make outfield play
difficult in left field in the afternoon
"The future ain't what it used to be"
Recent developments in
      economics
      politics
      the world
      technology
      morality
have the future less promising than it was

They go on and on
Lawrence Peter "Yogi" Berra
was one smart individual
and a hellava ballplayer

Ted

September 28, 1941
82 years ago
the last day of
the baseball season
Ted Williams went
6 for 8 in a double header
to finish at .406
the last player
to hit .400
82 years ago

Sixteen years later
he hit .388 to win his
fifth batting championship
beating the runner-up
Mickey Mantle
by 23 points and
won his sixth and last
championship the year after
He won two triple crowns
(*Batting Average, Home Runs
and Runs Batted In*)
in 1942 and 1947
and in his career he had
the highest batting average
and most home runs and RBIs
of any player who played
in those years – he had
a Triple Crown career

What was the most remarkable
was the fact that he lost
parts of 5 years to military service
in World War II and Korea,
landing a burning jet in Korea,
getting pneumonia in the process

Another American hero
Colonel (*and astronaut*) John Glenn
called baseball hero Williams
"The best wingman I ever had"

Williams is also the only man
in both the Baseball Hall of Fame
and the Fly Fishing Hall of Fame

It is fashionable today
to call people GOATs
"The Greatest of All Time"

I never saw Ty Cobb,
Babe Ruth, or Rogers Hornsby

All I can say is that
Theodore Samuel Williams
is the best I ever saw!

Teddy Ballgame and My Brother

My brother, Robert but "Bud" or "Buddy" to all who knew him, was sixteen years older than me and a nut-Red Sox fan.

Since we lived in New York City, the fan attachment might seem strange but he spent his sixth grade year in Boston living with my grandmother while my father transitioned from an Account Executive in a brokerage firm that failed to his father's firm – NYPD.

Idolizing my brother who left the family roof when I was two to join a religious order, I grew up a Red Sox fan also.

My father's best friend's brother-in-law was Jack Fadden, Red Sox trainer, and it was not long before an official American League baseball showed up at my house with the inscription *"To Brother McMullen – Ted Williams"* and the ball became my brother's most prized possession, travelling with him as he moved from one teaching assignment to another.

When I was nine years old, I became ill with a serious case as asthmatic bronchitis and was in bed for three weeks, missing school and miserable. My brother came to visit and, sitting on the edge of my bed, said *"I want you to have this"* and handed me the Ted Williams ball.

Knowing how much he prized the ball, I demurred, even saying *"It has your name on it"* but he resisted, saying *"Ok, then you keep it for me"* – and I did.

I grew up and even had him for a professor at Iona College *(two well-deserved A's and he threw me out of class once – I did not tell my mother)*.

We both moved on -- I married and he became the principal of Power Memorial High School where a student named Ferdinand Lewis Alcindor *(later Kareem Abdul Jabbar)* was the star of the basketball team.

We moved on more – He left the religious order, married, and taught at another college while I divorced and re-married. – and our families vacationed together. The ball travelled with me and Ted Williams remained our favorite player of all time although I had moved on to become first a New York Giant fan, then a New York Met one and, finally, a plain New York fan *(Mets & Yankees)*.

He remained a staunch Red Sox fan – so staunch that when he and I and our wives were at Dave Righetti's no-hitter against the Red Sox on July 4th, 1982 and my wife Barbara asked him just before the last Red Sox hitter of the game, Wade Boggs, came to the plate. *"Aren't you rooting for the no-hitter now?"*, he ignored her – when Boggs struck out, he wouldn't talk to her for over an hour.

Then he died in 2004 and I decided to put the ball in his coffin but, when I went to get it, the sun, through a skylight over it, had faded the inscription away – so I kept it.

Ted passed away two years before my brother and I can only hope that when Bud got to his destination, he got to meet his idol. I also hope that someday *(far in the future)*, I will see both of them – my two idols
Robert John McMullen *– the best person I ever knew …* and
Theodore Samuel Williams *– the best hitter I ever saw.*

Johnny Lujack Is Dead

Johnny Lujack is dead
at age 98
one of the heroes
of my young life

He was a quarterback
an All American quarterback
for Notre Dame
"The Fighting Irish"
New York City's
favorite football team
even though they were located
in South Bend Indiana

It was a different time then
Pro Football had not
yet begun its ascendancy
and no New York area colleges
had football teams

BUT
Notre Dame's games were
on the radio every Saturday
and they played in Yankee Stadium
every year against Army

In a heavily Irish New York
Notre Dame had
tremendous fan support
with the many fans known
as the "Subway Alumni"

Lujack became the quarterback in 1943
when his predecessor Angelo Bertelli
went into the Armed Forces
he played that season
and then went into the Armed Forces
himself not returning until 1946

How difficult must it have been
to return from chasing
German submarines
in the English Channel
to play college football?

but he did it well winning
the Heisman Trophy in 1947

Then it was off to the
National Football League
playing for the Chicago Bears
setting a single game passing record
in a very short four year career
cut short by a leg injury

He became a coach
then a broadcaster
and then went out
of the public view

In my 8-year-old youth
every time I threw
a pass with a football
I was Johnny Lujack

New York football
fans knew the name
Lujack
just as baseball fans
knew the name
DiMaggio
and they are both gone

Poetry Became My New Basketball

From the time
I was twelve
to over sixty
basketball was
the one constant
in my life

It took me through
changes in
      schools
      aspirations
      careers
      marriages
      parenthood
      residences

I was small in
high school and
only grew too late
to play in college

That didn't stop me though
I played
      for Catholic CYO teams
      for a local Episcopal church
      in a league at the Jewish Y
      in leagues on Wall Street,
        Westchester, and Inwood
      and pickup wherever I could
        get a game

I went from a
  fair player
   to a
  pretty good one
   to a
  good one
   to a
  very good one
   back to a
  good one
   and then a
  fair one
   and then
  done!

I only consulted, taught and
wrote columns on technology
for about 5 years and then,
through a quirk, poetry
  entered my life
  grabbed me by the throat
  and consumed me

Other than my wife and children
it became the number one thing
in my life

In short, it has became the basketball
of my mature life

But wait!

Basketball gave me
what's known medically
as "ARFURA"
"A Really Fucked Up Right Ankle"
    No tendons or ligaments
    Arthritis
    Bone spurs -- that won't keep me out of the Army
    And caused a ruptured tendon in my leg

Additionally I have had
    Two minor knee operations
    Jelly pumped into both knees annually
    Arthritis in both hips

While it was all worth it
basketball has crippled my body

Will poetry
do the same to my brain?

Obsession

Since I began writing what I
(and hopefully others) consider
poetry, it has become an obsession
with me. I read it and write it
constantly (albeit, some of the writing
is only in my head as I drive).

Perhaps it is because I came to
poetry rather late in life –
-- after years of non-fiction
writing about technology.

Perhaps it is because poetry
helps me search for truths
within me that I have only
recently come to accept.

Perhaps – oh, who the hell knows?

One of my favorite poets, Sharon Olds,
has been quoted as saying
*"I find not writing poems to be
much harder than writing them."*

Damn straight!

She writes well.
I hope that I do too
but, whatever the verdict,
I shall continue

Poetry Readings

I read poetry
A lot now
—here—and
other places

At the conclusion
of each poem,
people smile and laugh
—even clap

When I finish all
the poems I read,
they do it again

This makes me
feel pretty good
—pretty good!

I'd feel really good
if they bought
the goddamn books!

Hell of A Way To Make A Living

In "Poetry 180,"
Billy Collins disagrees with
the great Joyce Carol Oates,
attributing to her the belief that
"the number of poetry readers
in this country is about the same
as the number of people who
write poetry."

Collins believes that it is LESS!

I guess that I won't pay the rent
this way! Oh, well!

Submission

Dear Editor,

Enclosed are a few poems
which I sincerely hope
that you will choose to publish
in your fine journal.

In the event that you choose
not to do so, I hope that
your rag goes up in flames,
all your subscribers die, and
you and your staff rot in hell.

Respectfully submitted,

Why I Write

I write prose to, hopefully, help others
understand what I understand --
the rigor of writing the prose also
helps me understand the subject better.
Poetry is very different!
I write poetry to help me
understand myself -- my feelings,
my relations with people and with the world.
I hope you like the poetry that I write--
but, if you don't, I really don't care.

Poems Are Made ...

Poems are made
by fools like me
but only God
can make a flood
to destroy all
the peoples of the earth
except Noah
(*Genesis 6:21 7*)

Only God can send
fire and sulfur
from heaven
to destroy cities
and all the inhabitants
(*Genesis 19.4 12*)

Only God can
"harden the Pharaoh's heart"
so that he will chase the Israelites
 and give God an excuse
to send a tidal wave
to drown the Egyptian Army.
(*Exodus 14:11 14 – 15:17 20*)

God is one scary son-of-a-bitch.
How do I know?
The Bible told me so!

My Luck Holds!

Once again my luck seems to hold
I'm in my urologist's office
for a test but I have a chest pain
he takes my blood pressure
and it's through the roof

He cancels the test
and sends me right to the hospital
I'm there from Monday to Friday
I have a stent put in
to bypass a clogged artery
and I'm scheduled for the
a valve repair or replacement

If I hadn't been in
his office
I would have
just blown
off the pain

All my life
I've been very lucky
just being in the right place
at the right time
It has determined
      my profession
      my life partner
      the focus of our business
      and made me a writer,
      college professor and poet
in short, as Rocky Graziano
once said
"Somebody up there likes me"

Once more it seems
that my luck
has gotten me
through a crisis

The main questions
now are
　　　will it continue?
　　　and for how long?

The Miracles of Technology

A month ago I had a stent
put in near my heart
it was done through
an incision in my wrist
and I went home the next day

Last week I had a valve
put in near my heart
it was done through
two incisions in my groin
and I went home the next day

I was sent home
with a cardiac monitor
attached to my chest
and a modified cell phone
that would transfer my readings
to a service that would
then transfer them to my
medical group

Years ago
these procedures
would have meant
cutting into my chest
and an extended hospital stay

These technological miracles
aren't limited to medicine
think of our town government
where
        taxes and fees are paid online
        the Board Meetings are watchable online
        Board Members and officials are reachable via e-mail
        Meeting Agendas are available on-line
those who yearn for "*the good old days*"
should rather appreciate the "*here and now*"!

Magic of Technology

I was into technology early
as a programmer and manager
back in the days when there were
only mainframe computers

Then after 14 years
working for others
my wife, Barbara, and I
formed our own
consulting firm

We expected to
continue working
in the securities industry
on large systems

But through a
real stroke of luck
I purchased an Apple II
when there was little
software for it

When a few months
later VisiCalc
the first spreadsheet ever
was introduced and
we obtained an early copy

Our whole business changed
as we became
the Apple II VisiCalc experts
and installed systems
for clients ranging from

our local deli to major corporations
and foreign governments

There were constant
technology changes
the IBM PC arrived
then the Compaq Portable
then the Macintosh
and the iPhone
soon everybody had a laptop
and our business flourished
leading us into writing
for technology magazines
and teaching at colleges

Technology became
a staple of our lives
at home and office
filled with computers
of all sizes and makes
tablets galore and
an Amazon Echo
network tying together
three floors

To say that I was
not intimidated by
the magic of technology
would certainly be
an understatement

UNTIL
I was wheeled into
the Operating Room
of a major NYC hospital

There were
machines everywhere
Giant Machines
Mid-size machines
Small machines
it was overwhelming

It was like being in
a combination of
what I envision
a NASA control center
and a Star Wars set to be

Soon a dozen medical workers
began to perform tasks
on my body preparing me
for a surgical procedure
once again unbelievable!

After 60 years in technology
I was finally taken aback by it
God, this is impressive
truly the Magic of Technology

I never want to see it again!

Postscript
I was sent home
with a cardiac monitor
attached to my chest
and a modified cell phone
that would transfer my readings
to a service that would
then transfer them to my
medical group

I repeat:
it was mind blowing
to this Apple II user

However
I wish that I never
had the occasion
to learn about it

BUT
Once that I had
the occasion
I was oh so grateful
that it existed

He Stepped Up

Wally Pipp was the first baseman
for the New York Yankees –
-- a good first baseman.
One day he had a headache
and asked the manager
"to put the rookie in today".
He did and Pipp never
started another game
for the Yankees
for the rookie
Lou Gehrig stepped up!

Chad Mitchell was the
lead singer of the
Chad Mitchell Trio
He left the group to
seek greater stardom
as a soloist.
You may have heard of his
replacement with the group
John Denver stepped up!

When the recently acquired
Bobby Thomson broke his leg
in spring training with the
Milwaukee Braves, it opened
the door for a rookie.
Henry Arron stepped up!

When John The Baptist
lost his head, it was truly
a terrible thing
but the next guy
stepped up.

Perfection

I do many things well
(*if I may say so myself*);
I even do some things very well
and I do some things not-so-well
(*ask my wife*).

But even for most of the things
that I do very well,
I do not do perfectly.

There is always something about
most efforts (*even this poem*)
that could be done better.

I know – because, at times,
I have done some things perfectly
-- well, at least one thing.

I have faked my defender,
dribbled into the corner,
turned and gone up in the air,
released --- and ---
gotten nothing but net!

As the ball drops through
and I start back down the court,
I know that there is nothing
that I could have done better
at that instant.

If only I could get that same
feeling from many more things.
Life is more than a jump shot.

I Lit Gordon McRae's Cigarette

I was standing at the bar
in a restaurant in Shea Stadium
after a World Series game in 1969
I lit a cigarette (*you could smoke
in bars then*) as I tried to figure
out why no money was changing
hands over the bar.

Just then, the fellow next to me asked
me for a light and, as I turned to light
his cigarette, I recognized that it was
Gordon McRae who had song the
national anthem before the game

Over Gordon's head, I saw Joe DiMaggio
talking to Earl Warren at the end of the bar
and I realized that I was not in the public
restaurant. It turned out that I was in the
private club of the owner of the Mets
So I stayed

But I did not want to just sound like a fan
so I did not tell Gordon how much I liked
him in the movie version of Oklahoma

I also did not tell him how much I despised
the State of Oklahoma, having spent five
long years there between January 1962 and
April 1962 while in the Army.

It was only four months?
Well, it felt like five years!

Lawton was the third largest city
in the state and had no industry
other than Fort Sill where I was.
It had
> Bars (many)
> Private clubs
> Hotels
> Clip Joints
> Girls

Anything that could separate a
GI from his meager wages

It was a divided city with
> A Mexican section
> An Indian section
> A Black section
> A White Soldier section
> A White Real People's section

And for the first time this New Yorker
saw institutionalized segregation and
bigotry

About 25 years later, I met a woman
from Lawton and told her of black members
of my unit being refused service in a bar
where I was (I left with them)

I then said "*I'm sure that things have changed
in the last twenty-five years*" and she responded
"*Not so much*"

I told Gordon none of this
I just lit his cigarette.

Ghosts

When I think of
old radio shows
or sports oddities
I want to call
Mike Ryan
I can't call him
I gave the eulogy
at his funeral

When I think
profound or
deeper thoughts
I want to call
my older brother
the idol of my youth
I can't call him
I was a pallbearer
at his funeral

As I get older
I seem to conjure
thoughts of my
father and mother
more often – they
are also no longer
with us physically

The real ghosts --
and ghosts are real
-- they are not the
Caspers or the visitors
of Jacob Marley --
they are the spirits
who live within our
thoughts and memories

They bring smiles and
sadness and yearnings

As long as their memories
exist in us, they are real
and we are better for
their existence

Mike

Michael Robert Ryan
was my best friend
for a very long time
we had mutual interests
books – radio – sports
and a shared taste for beer

We talked constantly
      in the park
      at the bar
      on the phone (*probably for a total of many months' time over the years*)

Knowing nothing about computers
when graduating from college
and having no interest in knowing
we both spent all of our working lives
working with them

We worked together
for two firms
and good turns
and bad turns
did not destroy
our friendship

He had red hair
a quick smile
a terrific Irish tenor voice
would sing *Danny Boy*
both at any request and
at every wedding of my
friends (and mine)

I was his best man
and gave the toast
at his wedding and
the eulogy at his funeral
(another victim of Joe Camel)

Irish Voice

I used to get angry or,
at least, perturbed
when my wife, of Philadelphia
birth and German-Polish heritage
(there was a nasty combination of
which neither family approved – but
the union produced a Goddess),
would refer to me as "Irish"

"I'm not Irish", I would bellow,
"I'm American!"
The Irish killed each other for religious
reasons, used the feast of a Catholic
saint as an excuse to get drunk and foolish
(as if we needed an excuse)
and were just generally disreputable.
I refused to wear green on St. Patrick's
Day and generally disavowed my heritage.

I knew little of this heritage other than the
fact that the British had over run them and
made them part of the Empire – but they had
done that to the Canadians, Australians, Indians,
(and they hadn't become objects of jokes and
ridicule). I didn't understand the difference
between the Revolution and the Civil War,

In short, I might as well have been a Brit.

Of course, I grew up in an Irish Catholic
neighborhood, thanked the Maker that my
four grandparents got on the boat in Ireland,
drank in all the bars, listened to Ruthie
Morrissey sing songs of rebellion at
Mickey Carton's Mayo House in Rockaway,
and behaved like all the rest of "the micks"

It was only when I began to read the poetry
and literature of Moore, Synge, Yeats, and Thomas
that I began to feel the culture that already flowed
through my veins; when I read Bernadette Devin
writing of the present day economic inequities, my
anger boiled; and, when I read the works of the
McCourts, I began to understand from whence
I came.

So, if you're not Irish, I respect your heritage
but "*I'm sorry for your troubles*"

So I Had A Birthday

I got well wishes from
 family
 close friends
 Facebook friends
A close friend even wrote
a poem for the occasion
 "Birthday Sonnet"

Birthday questions used to be
 will the next year be even better than the last?
 will my health hold up for another year?
 will my friends and family have a good year?
Now the more pressing questions are
 will the country survive?
 will the world survive?

Do you know the answers?
I, sure as hell, don't

This Old House

In 1954
just before the
rock 'n' roll explosion
Rosemary Clooney
had a number one hit
"This Ole House"
we normally remember it
as *This Old House*

I was then living in a
New York City Apartment
I never thought of
living in a house
certainly not an old one
but I liked the song

Now I live in an
almost 300-year-old
converted barn
with
      a wife
      a dog
      and two cats
and wouldn't
have it any other way

When I first got married
I wanted to live in a
New York City Apartment
my new bride
a Philadelphia Princess
said "**No way!**"

It's funny how
our visions change

Longevity

In the first almost 40 years of my life, I lived in:
— 4 Inwood Apartments (I only remember 3; the first was birth to under 2).
— 3 Army barracks (all in 6 months)
— 3 Riverdale Apartments
— 1 Westchester cottage on an estate

In the almost 44 years since. I've lived in:
— 1 Jefferson Valley, NY house

I guess I've settled in

Getting Older

More aches & pains
than ever before
and that's not all
>*excuse me – what did you say?*
>no more jump shots
>*what was that guy's name who ....?*
>more naps
>*do you think I need my cane?*
>it takes 10 minutes to take the daily pills

but
>considering the alternatives ...

Backup

My Books are on my Kindle,
My Addresses are in the Cloud
My Calendar is in Google
and Gmail has my mail.

My writing is on my Computer,
My pictures are in Flickr,
My music is on Amazon
And my thoughts are on the Web.

All these are "backed up";
I am not
When my power goes out,
I do too

We Live To Die

We live to die;
this we cannot deny.

But we do deny
that we live to die.
We want to live
...to laugh
... to cry
.....to love
......to fuck
......to read
.......to sing
........to dance
.........to learn

But, in the end,
what we have learned
is that we lived to die;
this we could not deny.

Important People

Over the years
through no fault
of my own I have
been around many
important people

I have
     held Eleanor Roosevelt's coat
     lit Gordon McRae's cigarette
     talked baseball with Casey Stengel
     talked football with Weeb Eubank
     exchanged pleasantries with Pearl Bailey
     basked in the presence of Lena Horne
     interviewed Steve Jobs
     discussed history with Arthur Schlessinger, Jr.
     been in a room with Lauren Bacall
     reminisced about my late father with
          ex-NYC Mayor Bob Wagner
     talked writing with George Plimpton
             and David Halberstrom
     speculated about technology with Bill Gates
     talked basketball and politics with Gov. George Pataki

BUT
The most important person
with whom I have ever
spent any time with is
Barbara E McMullen
my wife of 45 years

Tombstones In My Mind

(people, not mentioned in the book, and no longer with us, who impacted my life)

Bill McLoughlin, Sr
Bill Mcloughlin, Jr
John Muccia
Bob Cummings
Warren Hennessey
Bob Arco
Gloria Vann Arco
Joe Conway
Dave Cawley
Rick Maass
Cathy Sheehan
Pat Tonry Roach
Mike Passarella
Charles While, CSP
George Hagmeir, CSP
Kevin Devine, CSP
Michael Fitzgibbon, FSC
Bill Swiacki
Carlo Evangelsti
Jeff Collier
Walter Ludman, Sr
Arthur McCarroll

EA Walsh, FSCH
MF Bradley, FSCH
JM Egan, FSCH
ED McKenna, FSCH
RB Power, FSCH
Jim "Hobart" Lambert
Ellen Mulderrig
Rita Fahey O'Sullivan
Andrew Greeley
Daniel Berrigan, SJ
George Glansman, SJ
Jim McArdle
Bob Gorman
John Guinan
Bill Fleming
Steve Fearon
Sr. Mary Redempta
Terry Dugan
Larry Heiser
Arthur Monsees
Nellie Ludman
Ann McCarroll

Bob Donohue
Charles Milau
Dr. Joseph McDonald
Beatrice McMullen
Francis Crilley
Frances Crilley
Francis Crilley, Jr
Edith Crilley
George Davidsohn
Bob Scales
Rita McQuade
Judy Holder Trust
William F Buckley, Jr
Jim Guinan
Sandra Irizzary Ward
Jacqueline Wolf Birch
John Taaffe
John Slevin
Carole Collier Blanc
Susan Crilley Peckol
Margaret McMullen
Mary Agnes Shea

Afterward

The aforementioned are those who immediately come to mind (*I seem to think of my brother and Mike every day*) and, while it is important to remember them, it is at least as important to give credit to those who are with us today (*and, hopefully. will continue to be*). I will list many here (*and, unfortunately, forget some*):

- The remaining Inwood crew – Dan, Jim, Frank, Tod, Gene, Terry, Artie, Chick and the *Isham Street contingent* (Denis, Richie, Leo, and John V)
- The Cardinal Farley roommates – Richie Donnelly, Jorge Mascaro, and the two Mikes, Cohalan and Horowitz
- Those who give me a regular stage to read my poetry, while learning from other writers – Vinny Dacquino, David Leo Sirois, Ralph Nazareth, Bill Buschel, Jerry Johnson, Janet Kuypers, John Kaprielian, and Craig Lyvers
- The talented writers who come regularly to my "home group", the Mahopac Writers Group ("*Vinny's group*") – Priscilla (*who lights up every group she belongs to*), Rusty, Don, Theresé, Bryan, the "eens" (*Kathleen & Maureen*), Lori, Andy, the Bobs (Lee & Z), George, Sonia, Lenny, Cristina, Joe, & Miriam
- Others from my journey along the way who are still on the "*speed dial*" – John Coffey, Norman Adams, Bob Flanagan, Jack May, Bill Merlino, Jim Finn, Carol McLoughlin, Bob Clark, Dave Savage, John Lafferty, Herb Roseman, & "Son" Sullivan.
- The Yorktown Town Supervisors who have listened to my Poet Laureate readings – Michael Grace, Ilan "Lanny" Gilbert. Matt Slater, & Tom Diana
- The demanding pets who keep me busy every day – Fala The Wonder Dog, Ninja the Stealth Cat, Coco The Wild Ever-Kitten, & Juliet The Hungry Deer

And, of course, once again -- Barbara, Claire, & Luke

About the Author

John F. McMullen is a graduate of Iona College and holds two Masters degrees from Marist College (MSCS and MPA). He is the Poet Laureate of the Town of Yorktown, NY, the author of over 2,500 columns and articles and twelve books, ten of which are collections of poetry (*his most recent "**My Life in 25 Poems**" is available at Amazon as are all the others*), and was the host of a weekly Internet Radio Show (*300 shows in the series*).

Made in United States
North Haven, CT
21 November 2023

44342526R00075